RESTART FLUTE

Written by Clarissa Payne

WISE PUBLICATIONS
part of The Music Sales Group

London / New York / Paris / Sydney / Copenhagen / Berlin / Madrid / Hong Kong / Tokyo

Published by
Wise Publications
14-15 Berners Street, London W1T 3LJ, UK.

Exclusive Distributors:
Music Sales Limited
Distribution Centre, Newmarket Road,
Bury St Edmunds, Suffolk IP33 3YB, UK.
Music Sales Pty Limited
20 Resolution Drive, Caringbah, NSW 2229, Australia.

Order No. AM1002815
ISBN: 978-1-84938-972-3
This book © Copyright 2012 Wise Publications,
a division of Music Sales Limited.

Author: Clarissa Payne.
Project editor: Lizzie Moore.
Book design: Camden Music.
Photography: Matthew Ward.
Flute played by Howard McGill.
CD mixed and mastered by Jonas Persson.
Cover design by Tim Field.
Cover photograph courtesy of Robert Kneschke - Fotolia.

Printed in the EU.

**For access to the complementary piano accompaniments for this book,
go to www.hybridpublications.com and enter the code BM733.**

Introduction

Congratulations! You've made a great decision to get going again with the flute. The benefits of learning an instrument are now widely known; as well as the great pleasure of playing and improving, research suggests that studying music can improve your problem-solving abilities, boost your self-esteem and help you to relax and deal with stress.

This book isn't a beginner's method—it's assumed that you've reached around grade 4 or 5 standard in the past and that you already know a bit about technique and notation. But don't panic; there are lots of reminders along the way as well as reference charts at the back of the book, and you'll probably be surprised how quickly it all comes flooding back.

Let's not forget that you're doing this because *you* want to, not because you're being made to. So you already have the most important thing you need: the motivation to put in the hard work necessary to progress.

Now you've dug out your flute from the cupboard, where to start? First things first. If it has been lying unplayed for a few years it may well need a service. Ask in your local woodwind shop; they may have an in-house repairer or be able to recommend one. It's really worth doing this so that your progress isn't compromised by a faulty instrument, which can be very frustrating. If you're not sure, ask a local teacher.

After all, you will be needing one—while this book contains plenty of advice and clear illustrations to guide you, nothing beats individual feedback from an experienced professional. Again, your local woodwind shop should keep a register of teachers, as should your library (or you could look online). Maybe you have children who learn an instrument. If so, ask their teacher for a recommendation.

The 12 different pieces in this book cover a range of styles and present various technical challenges. Treat them as keys to the knowledge that you already have about playing the flute and about aspects of music in general. Before each one is a short summary to remind you what to look out for, along with an exercise to help you prepare for the piece.

Refresher

Just before you give the pieces a go, here's a quick refresher on the basics of flute playing.

Breathing

You're probably dying to put the flute together and get going, but just before you do, another reminder about the most important thing of all—**air**. As the bow is to the violinist, so the airstream is to us.

Take a piece of paper roughly 4 x 3cm and hold it horizontally against the wall in front of your lips while you stand about 5cm away. Keep your shoulders and neck relaxed and take a deep breath, dropping your jaw and drawing the air into your abdomen. Start blowing against the paper and at the same time let go of it.

The beauty of this exercise is that there can't be any doubt if you're doing it right or wrong! You're aiming to keep the paper pinned against the wall with as little flapping about as possible. Once you've got it, time yourself and try to beat your record. Of course, if you feel dizzy, stop and sit down.

These photos show how you breathe using your diaphragm and not your chest. Make sure you keep your shoulders down.

 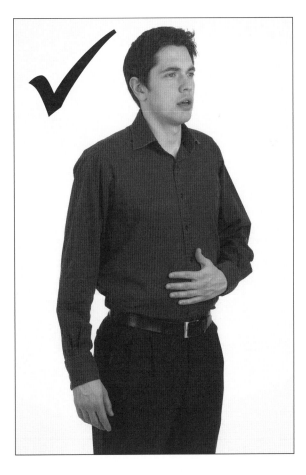

You could also try blowing up a balloon or blowing bubbles in a glass of water with a straw. It's important to keep the throat relaxed and open. Try whispering a long 'ahhhhh' and noticing how the throat feels.

Posture

It's impossible to think about breathing without also thinking about posture. Let's draw another analogy with stringed instruments. A cello or violin has a beautiful curved wooden resonating chamber, within which the sound waves can vibrate. We flute players only have a metal tube to blow across, unless we use our own bodies as our resonating chambers. So we need to make sure we have the biggest sound-box we can!

Maybe you have unhappy memories of being nagged by a childhood teacher to stand up straighter—well unfortunately the advice still stands. Let's start from the ground up. Stand on the floor (preferably in front of a mirror) with your feet roughly 20 or 30cm apart, then think 'knees above ankles, hips above knees, shoulders above hips'. You'll probably find yourself an inch or two taller. Hold your head up and, without rotating your body whether from the hips or the shoulders, turn your head roughly 45 degrees to the left. This is how we accommodate the inconvenient sideways nature of the flute!

Look at the photo below. This is a good example of the correct posture for playing your flute in a standing position.

Embouchure

The quickest way to remind yourself of the correct lip shape is to say aloud the syllable 'p'. A mirror is, again, extremely useful. Start with your lips shut and say a few 'p's. Have a look at the shape your lips make and the size of the embouchure. It should be central and small. Now say another 'p' and immediately start blowing an airstream like the one you used in the exercise with the piece of paper.

Finally, let's get the flute out. Take just the headjoint for the moment. It's really important at this stage to remember that the flute isn't magnetic—I've seen far too many students stand beautifully tall and straight, and then drop their head to come and meet the flute. It comes to you, not the other way around. Most people don't even realise they have this habit, which is why practising in front of a mirror is so worthwhile.

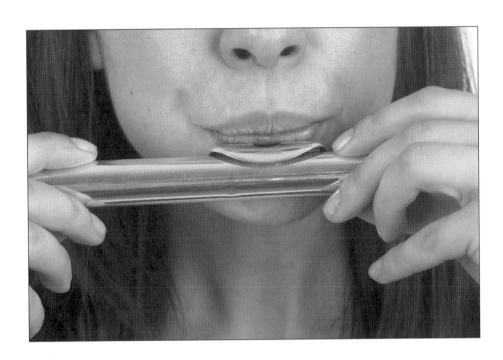

Your memory is probably kicking in and you've raised the flute to your lips without thinking about it, but if you want a reference point, the near edge of the embouchure hole should align with the bottom of your lower lip (see photo above). Imagine you're still blowing the piece of paper, take a deep breath and play a long note. Listen carefully—does it sound clean or is there a lot of surplus air around the sound?

As well as using your ears, you can use your eyes to see if the embouchure is too large. Immediately after finishing your long note, take a look at the condensation on the lip-plate. Ideally it should form a neat triangle tapering away from the hole. If the condensation is over an area bigger than the hole, you're simply wasting air. Blowing over the solid metal won't produce any sound.

Assembly

Time to put the whole flute together again. No doubt you remember looking at the ingenious mechanism for the first time and wondering how it all worked. This system, invented in the 19th century by Theobald Boehm, is so sturdy and effective that it's hardly changed since then. However, we do still have to look after it.

When you put the flute together and take it apart, take care to hold it by the body, **not on any of the rods or keys**. When you've finished playing, always clean the flute. That way your instrument will stay in top condition and last a lot longer between services.

Hand Position

Keep your shoulders, elbows and wrists relaxed as you lift the flute to your lips. The fingers should be curved and aiming for the centre of the keys. (If you have an open-holed flute you won't get away with anything else!) The left thumb rests on the thumb key slightly side-on—don't worry about trying to make a 90-degree angle. The right thumb should rest below the index finger—try not to make a hook shape that the flute could roll around in. Look at the following photos to see how to hold the flute and where your fingers should be on the keys.

Time to get stuck into some music. Listen out for the clicks counting you in.

Remember, all the pieces are recorded once with the flute part for you to listen, and once with the backing track only so that you can take the starring role.

William Tell Overture

This is a great piece with which to get going. Have a look at the reminders on key signature, time signature and note values, and then warm up with the articulation exercise.

Remember there is a fingering chart at the back of this book.

DO YOU REMEMBER?

Key signature

 This means that every B is a B♭. This piece is in F major.

Time signature

 This means that there are two crotchet beats in each bar. Listen to the introduction and count along '1, 2 / 1, 2 / 1, 2 / 1, 2'

Note values

This piece uses three different **note values:**

crotchets: worth 1 beat   **minim:** worth 2 beats   **quavers:** worth ½ a beat

 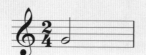 

Breath mark

✓ This symbol is used as a recommendation for a breath.

Articulation

The 'French School' of the turn of the 19th and 20th centuries is often considered the foundation of the way that we play today. Try searching for Paul Taffanel, Philippe Gaubert, Marcel Moyse and Jean-Pierre Rampal on YouTube or Spotify. However, the French may well have an unfair advantage—think of the way a French person pronounces 'tu' as opposed to an English-speaker's 'tea' and 'toast'. With 'tu', the tongue is further forward and the throat is more open. Try the exercise below:

Play This First

Keep the airstream strong (as if blowing the piece of paper against the wall) and the tongue movement small.

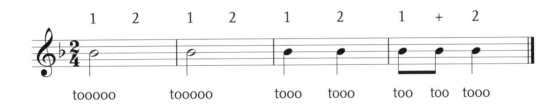

William Tell Overture

Composed by Gioacchino Rossini

Allegro vivace

The Can Can

Play This First

Practise these scales first to help you to play the piece:

C major

G major

The Can Can

Music by Jacques Offenbach

Allegro

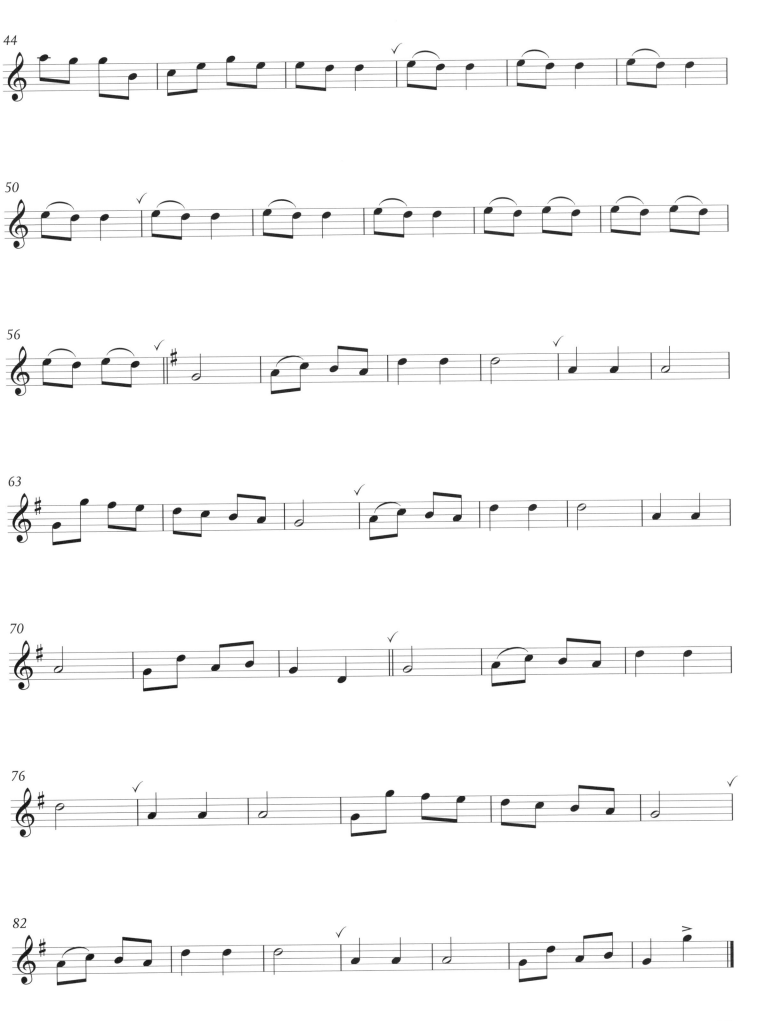

Moon River

This beautiful tune, famously featured in *Breakfast At Tiffany's*, was written by the film composer Henry Mancini, who also wrote the *Pink Panther* theme. When practising the warm-up exercise, try for your sweetest singing sound, and think of the vowel shape 'oooooo'.

DO YOU REMEMBER?

Triplet

 Play these three notes equally in the space of a crotchet.

Time signature

 This means that there are three crotchets in a bar.

D.S. al Coda

This means go back to the sign 𝄋, then when you reach ⊕, jump to the **Coda**.

Key signature

 This piece is in F major, which is the same key we played in for 'William Tell', our first piece in the book. Remember to make sure every B is a B♭.

rall.

This means to gradually get slower to the ⌒ pause, where we hold on the last note for longer than usual. If you are playing with the backing track, hold the note until the backing finishes.

Play This First

This will help to create smooth, slurred interval leaps from note to note. You will find a lot of these wide, slurred intervals in the piece. Make sure your breathing is controlled.

Play with a singing sound.

Before you get stuck into this piece, play through bars 49–62 (see below). The flute part in these bars plays the countermelody rather than the melody. This means that the flute does not play the tune here and so needs to be quieter than the main melody. It's worth practising this before you start, as it goes quite high and will need controlled breathing to keep the volume down.

Moon River

Words by Johnny Mercer & Music by Henry Mancini

That's Amoré

There are a couple of techniques featured in this tune which sound tricky, but aren't at all. They will definitely impress your audience.

Look for grace notes—they're smaller notes before, after or between the main notes that are played very quickly. The first one is in bar 10. Practise the tune *without* the grace notes first, then put them in, being careful to keep the same rhythm. It should sound as if you've just made them up on the spur of the moment! Listen to the CD to hear how it's done.

Can you see the **glissandos**? These are the straight diagonal lines between two notes. The first one is in bar 15. Imagine a trombonist pulling the slide in or out to join the two notes; that's the effect you're after. We don't have a slide, so we have to use our fingers to fill in all (or most) of the notes between the main ones. It's the effect you're after, not total perfection! Again, have a listen to get the idea.

DO YOU REMEMBER?

Key signature

This piece begins in A major and then changes key up to B♭ major. A lot of pop songs use this technique.

Time signature

 This means that there are three crotchets in a bar—waltz time!

Extra sharps and flats

 B♯: this is the same as C♮. It's written this way because C♯ is in the key signature.

DO YOU REMEMBER?

Grace notes and glissandos

Italian terms

rit. : this is short for *ritenuto*, and means slow down.

A tempo: back to the original speed.

cresc. : this is short for *crescendo*, and means get louder.

dim. : this is short for *diminuendo*, and means get quieter.

That's Amoré

Words & Music by Harry Warren & Jack Brooks

(accordion cue)

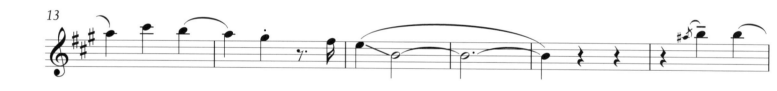

Theme From Mission: Impossible

Don't be phased by five beats in a bar. If you can count to two, three or four you can count to five!

There are two more articulations to practise here. Firstly, the **accent**. This is a note with a real punch to it, you need to expel the air fast from the diaphragm and then die away.

Do you remember how to play **staccato** notes? They're the ones with dots above or below (not to be confused with dotted notes, where the dot is beside the note and actually changes its length). Staccato notes are played extremely short and crisp, almost as if you are saying 'tut' while you play.

DO YOU REMEMBER?

Time signature

 This means that there are five crotchet beats in a bar.

Articulation markings

Dynamics

This piece is loud all the way through, we know this because of the repeated use of *f* (forte). It dies down at bar 26 where we see *mf* (mezzo forte) which means moderately loud. Be sure to play as loud as you can *ff* (fortissimo) from bar 70 to the end.

Play This First

Accent exercise

Accents are used to reinforce notes, as these are all accented, play them all with force.

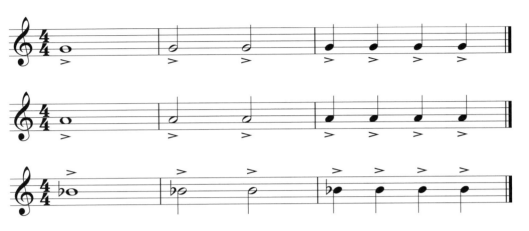

Staccato exercise

These 17 bars are quite tricky, so make sure you get your fingers round them before you tackle the piece as a whole.

Theme From Mission: Impossible

Music by Lalo Schifrin

Morning

So far we've been dealing with *simple time signatures*: $\frac{2}{4}$, $\frac{3}{4}$, $\frac{4}{4}$ and $\frac{5}{4}$.

Time for a review of *compound time signatures*.

As the name suggests, the beats in the bar are made up of three smaller beats.

Two ways to count

'Morning', which is the first movement from Edvard Grieg's famous *Peer Gynt* suite, is in $\frac{6}{8}$. As it is quite slow you can count the six *quaver* beats to be sure where you are, or count the two dotted crotchet beats for a more flowing feel.

You may well have remembered that when four is the bottom number in the time signature, we are dealing with crotchet beats, and when eight is on the bottom it's quavers.

Play This First

Aim for a sweet legato sound. Say 'oooooo' and then keep that shape inside your mouth and throat while you play. When you do start the piece, make sure you watch out for the different dynamics—from p to f and back again.

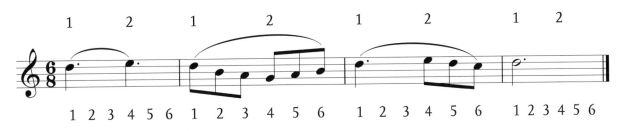

Morning

Composed by Edvard Grieg

Calmly

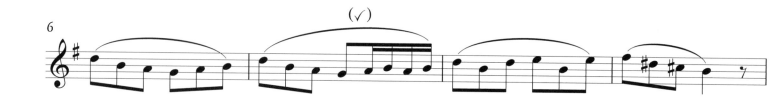

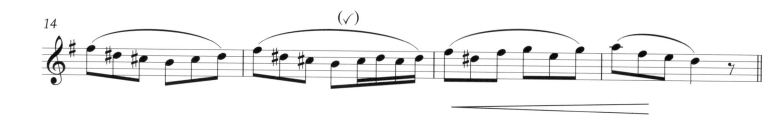

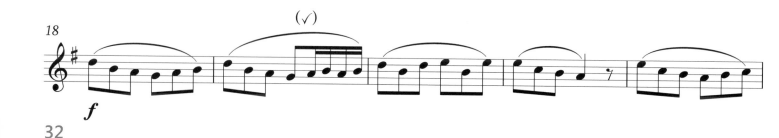

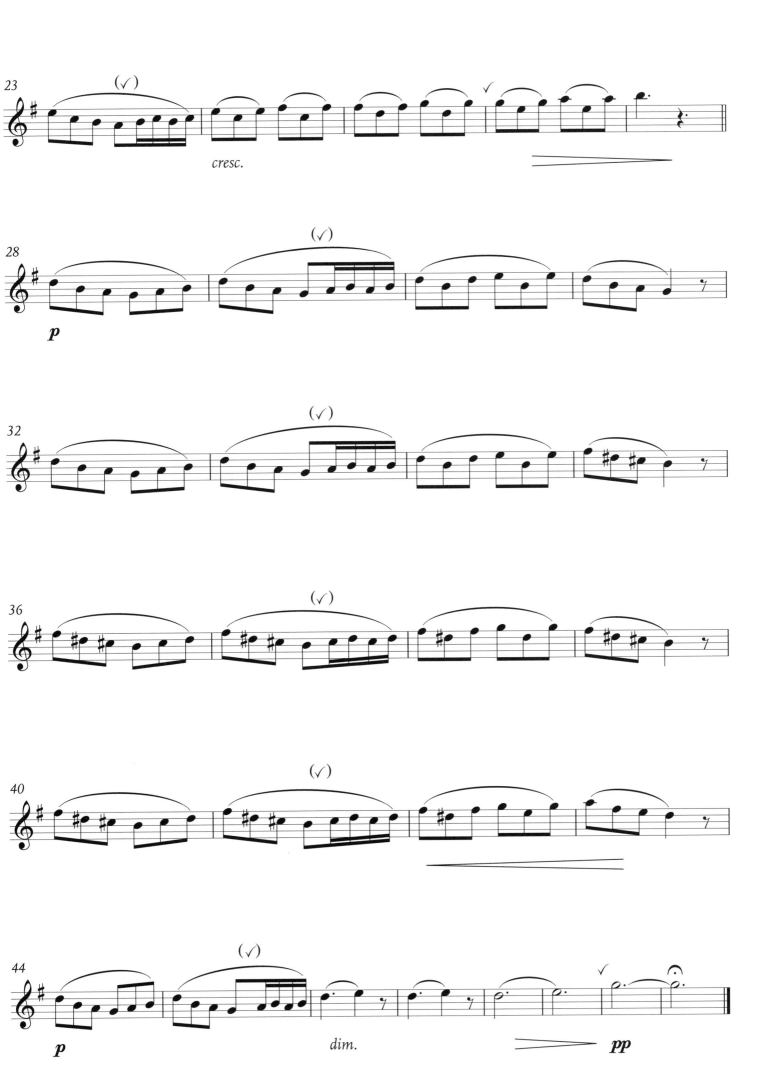

Hallelujah

This particular version of the song is sung by Alexandra Burke, but the original version was written and sung by Leonard Cohen. You will notice that there is a key change for the final verse and chorus. Watch out for this, it's very common in pop music.

We're staying with compound time signatures; this one is in **12/8**. Instead of two compound beats, there are four.

Play This First

To help get both keys under your fingers, practise these two scales before you begin.

Hallelujah

Words & Music by Leonard Cohen

Expressively ♩. = 61

mp cantabile

cresc. poco a poco

f

mf espress.

Big Spender

Time for a change of mood! Another one in $\frac{12}{8}$, this time with lots of flats thrown in to keep you on your toes. This one also needs the accents and staccatos you were practising for *Mission: Impossible*.

DO YOU REMEMBER?

Watch out for the structure here:

D.S. al Coda: go back to the sign 𝄋. Then:

to Coda ⊕: jump to the coda sign ⊕ at the end.

Italian terms

Marc. e poco stacc. : short for *marcato e poco staccato* which means emphasise each note, using a little staccato.

sfp ———— : This means to punch the note and die away quickly and then suddenly start to crescendo through the note. Listen to the demonstration on the CD to hear how this should sound.

Play This First

Play this chromatic scale before you begin the piece. You will find a lot of chromaticism throughout, so this should help get your fingers used to the patterns.

This one needs a big, 'brassy' sound. Say 'aaaaah' and then keep your mouth and throat in that shape while you play. You could also try increasing the air speed, and don't forget to support with your diaphragm. Listen to Shirley Bassey perform this song and try to sound as powerful as she does.

Big Spender

Words by Dorothy Fields & Music by Cy Coleman

D.S. al Coda

✆ Coda

The Lonely Goatherd

Back to a simple time signature now. Do you recognise these symbols?

short for
'common time'

short for
'split or cut common time'

We're in $\frac{2}{2}$ = two *minim* beats in a bar. This gives the piece a more lively and brisk feeling than counting four crotchets.

Play This First

To get the full yodelling effect, warm up with the exercise below. Don't forget to keep the throat open and think of singing 'aaaaah' while you play.

The Lonely Goatherd

Words by Oscar Hammerstein II & Music by Richard Rodgers

Oye Como Va

We'll use this salsa classic to revise a few features from earlier pieces. Look out for the accented staccato notes. There are also some *tenuto* notes.

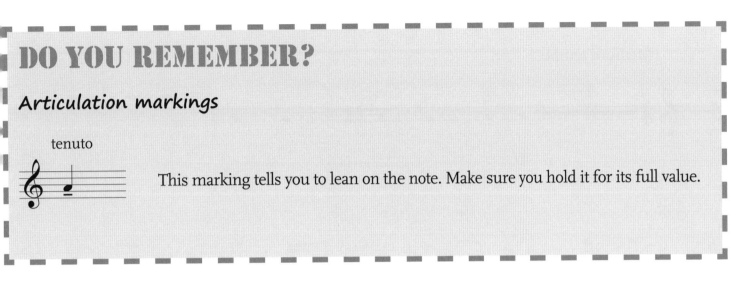

DO YOU REMEMBER?

Articulation markings

tenuto

This marking tells you to lean on the note. Make sure you hold it for its full value.

There's another chance to play glissandos, this time not between notes but falling away to nothing. Listen to the demonstration on the CD to get the idea.

There are more triplets to watch out for—they should slide across the beat.

Look carefully at the syncopated rhythms in bars 31–34 and 61–64.

Play This First

Practise these bars before you tackle the piece as they are heavily syncopated, slightly tricky and may take you by surprise!

Oye Como Va

Words & Music by Tito Puente

Medium tempo

(fall)

I Got Rhythm

This piece has two sections: one with *straight* quavers (played as written) and one with *swung* quavers. In jazz, the quavers are almost always swung. This means that the quaver *on* the beat is longer.

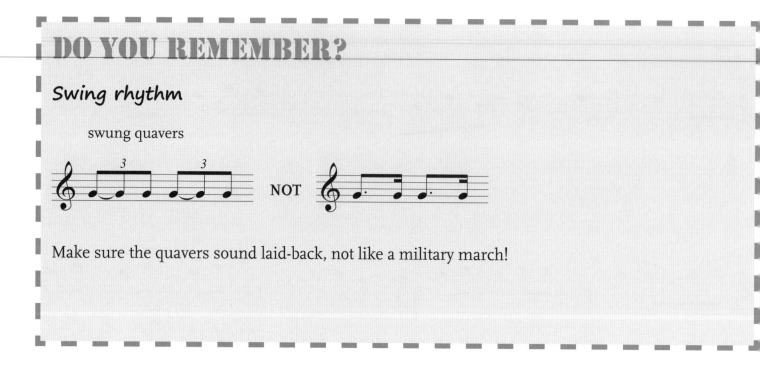

DO YOU REMEMBER?

Swing rhythm

swung quavers

NOT

Make sure the quavers sound laid-back, not like a military march!

Play This First

Have a go at this B♭ major scale using the knowledge you have just learnt from the section above. Be sure not to turn them into dotted quavers!

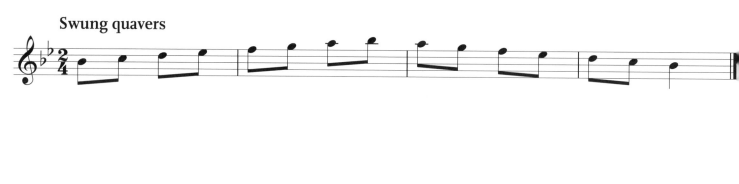

Swung quavers

50

I Got Rhythm

Music by George Gershwin

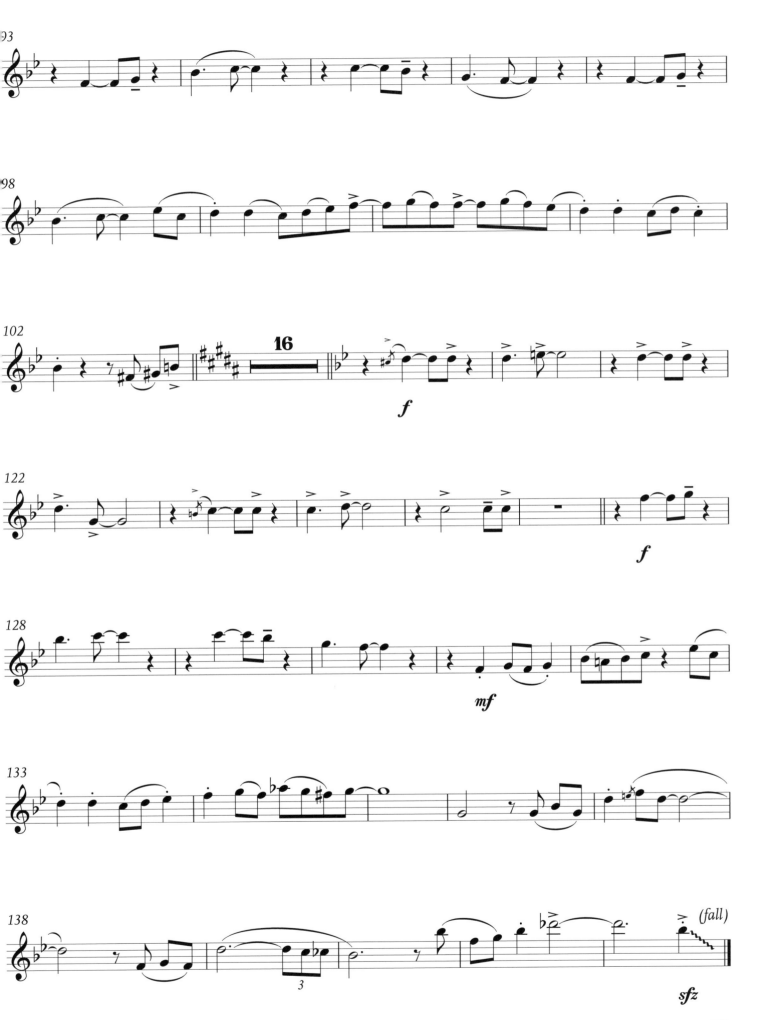

Super Trouper

Words & Music by Benny Andersson & Björn Ulvaeus

Well done! The pieces in this book should have given you quite a workout, and you're probably surprised at how much was still in the memory bank. Let's finish off with a bit of fun. Concentrate on using a bright, singing sound and making your articulation clean.

123456789

Theory Reminder

Accidentals (alter the pitch of notes)

♯   **Sharp:** raises the pitch of any note by a semitone

♭   **Flat:** lowers the pitch of any note by a semitone

♮   **Natural:** cancels out the effect of a sharp or flat

×   **Double Sharp:** raises the pitch of any note by a whole tone

♭♭   **Double Flat:** lowers the pitch of any note by a whole tone

Note values

○ ▬   **Semibreve:** (whole note), or rest of equivalent length, lasts for four beats

♩ ▬   **Minim:** (half note), or rest of equivalent length, lasts for two beats

♩ 𝄽   **Crotchet:** (quarter note), or rest of equivalent length, lasts for a quarter of a semibreve and is commonly used as a one-beat note

♪ 𝄾   **Quaver:** (eighth note), or rest of equivalent length, lasts for half a beat

♬ 𝄿   **Semiquaver:** (sixteenth note), or rest of equivalent length, lasts for a quarter of a beat

♬ 𝅀   **Demisemiquaver:** (thirty-second note), or rest of equivalent length, lasts for an eighth of a beat

♩. 𝄽·   **Dot:** increases the length of a note or rest by 50%

‿   **Tie:** joins two notes together — the duration of the second is added to the first

Time signatures

Simple time

$\frac{2}{4}$ 2 crotchet beats in a bar

$\frac{3}{4}$ 3 crotchet beats in a bar

$\frac{4}{4}$ 4 crotchet beats in a bar

$\frac{3}{2}$ 3 minim beats in a bar

Compound time

$\frac{6}{8}$ 6 quaver beats in a bar

$\frac{9}{8}$ 9 quaver beats in a bar

$\frac{12}{8}$ 12 quaver beats in a bar

Unusual time signatures

$\frac{5}{8}$ 5 quaver beats in a bar

$\frac{7}{8}$ 7 quaver beats in a bar

$\frac{11}{8}$ 11 quaver beats in a bar

Other useful terms

Adagio: slow, between andante and largo

Allegretto: moderately fast

Cadenza: a solo section, often used to show off musical technique within a Concerto or similar piece

Concerto: a piece in three parts consisting of a soloist accompanied by an orchestra

Dolce: sweet/gentle

Grazioso: gracefully

Grave: slow and solemn

Largo: very slowly

Lento: slowly

Meno: less

Minuet: a piece originally from a dance in triple time

Moderato: moderately

Mosso: with movement

Movement: section of a large composition (e.g. 3rd movement of symphony no. 5)

Ostinato: a short pattern that is repeated

Overture: a piece used as an introduction to a dramatic, choral or instrumental composition

Più: more

Presto: very fast

Rondo: a musical form in which one section comes back time and time again

Rubato: a flexible tempo that can be pulled around to suit the style

Sonata: instrumental piece for piano, or solo instrument and piano, usually in three movements

Stringendo: pressing forward or moving on

Subito, sub.: suddenly

Symphony: a large composition for orchestra often in four movements

Tempo: the speed of a piece of music

Troppo: too much

Tutti: all, used to indicate where everyone plays together

Vibrato: repeated slight change in pitch to a single note to make a richer sound

Vivace: lively and fast

Flute Fingering Chart

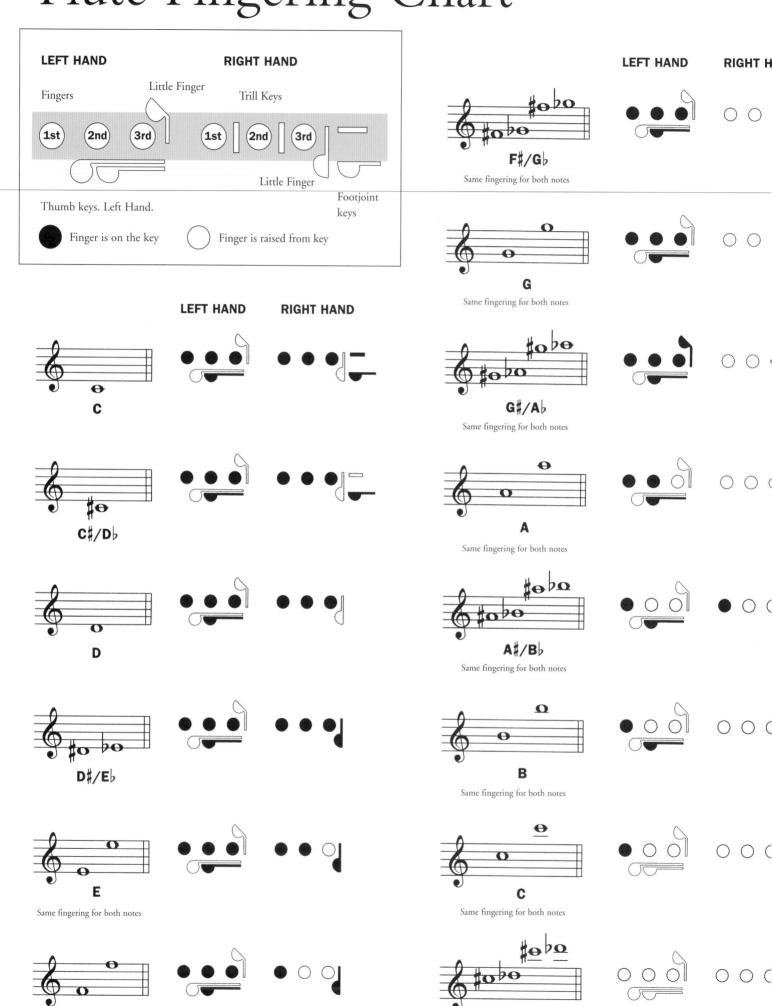

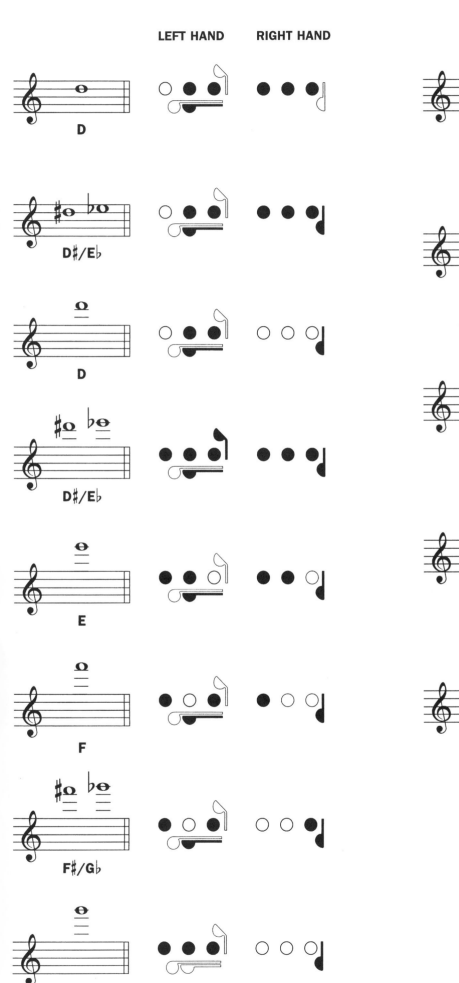

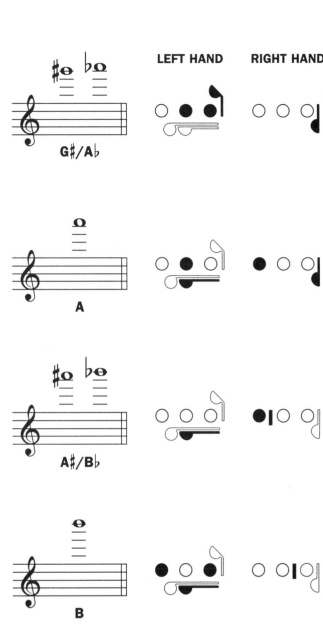

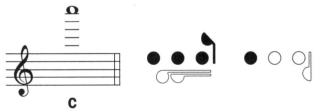

Notation

Dotted Double Bars

:‖ Repeat what appears between the beginning of the piece and the dotted double bar.

‖: :‖ Repeat what appears between the dotted double bars.

First and Second Endings

The first ending is played the first time through the passage; when the passage is repeated, the first ending is skipped and the second ending is played instead.

D.C. (Da Capo)

Return to the beginning of the piece.

D.C. al Fine

Return to the beginning and play to the indicated end (*Fine*). When playing a *D.C.* repeats are not taken and first endings are skipped.

D.S. (Dal Segno)

Return to the sign 𝄋

D.S. al Fine

Return to the sign 𝄋 and play to the indicated end (*Fine*).

D.S. al Coda

Play from the sign 𝄋 to the point at which ⊕ or *To Coda* appears; skip from there to the Coda. When playing a *D.𝄋.* repeats are not taken and first endings are skipped.

Repeat Signs

⅟ Repeat the preceding measure.

Subdivision

♪ Subdivide the note value into the smaller values indicated by the slash(es).

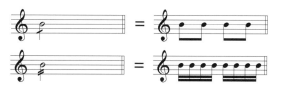

Two Instrument Parts on One Staff

Notes with stems *up* are played by the first player.

Notes with stems *down* are played by the second player.

The No. 1 indicates the first player, and the No. 2 the second player.

a2 (a due) indicates that both players play at once (in unison).

divisi indicates two separate parts written on the same staff.

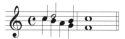

Rests

Full-measure rests: the block hanging from the fourth line indicates a full-measure rest in all time signatures. (The No. 1 is sometimes added for clarity.)

Any rest shorter than a full measure is written according to the time signature.

Two-measure rests: in any time signature these may be written as enlarged full-measure rests and labelled with the No. 2. Rests longer than 2 measures use the ensemble rest sign.

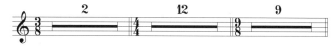

Instrument Care

Things to have on hand
Soft absorbent cloth (for outside).
Cleaning rod with soft cloth or handkerchief (for inside).
Medium-bristle artist's paintbrush.
Cork grease or vaseline.
Pencil with an eraser (bring to every rehearsal).

Putting the instrument together
Since the flute's key mechanism is quite
delicate (with keys and rods that are easily bent),
you should put it together and take it apart carefully.
Use a little cork grease or vaseline on the joints
only if necessary.

Grasp the main section of the flute and,
with a gentle twisting motion, ease the head joint
into position; do the same with the foot joint.

Cleaning
Keep the outside of the flute free of dust
and fingerprints by wiping it with a soft absorbent
cloth – remember that perspiration from the
player's hands will cause corrosion of the keys.
(*Never* use commercial metal polish.) Swab the inside
of the instrument thoroughly after every use,
using the cleaning rod and handkerchief.

An artist's paintbrush works well for
cleaning around the keys and beneath the rods.
An occasional drop of oil on the screws,
springs and moving parts will prevent rust and
sticking keys, but be sure not to get any on the pads.
All other maintenance processes (such as regulation
of the adjustment screws) are best left to the
professional repairman.

Storing
During short intermissions in rehearsals and
practice sessions, the flute may be rested on any
secure surface. Rest the instrument with the
keys facing upward so that collected moisture
will not reach the pads. Otherwise the flute
and piccolo should be in the player's hands or
in the case.

Transposition

The flute is not a transposing instrument;
it sounds the written pitch.
The piccolo sounds one octave above
the written pitch.

Written:

Sounds:

Pitch System

The letter names which appear at the top of the
fingering chart indicate the relative octave as well as
the name of each pitch, as shown below.

C² B²   C¹ B¹   C B   c b   c¹ b¹   c² b²   c³ b³   c⁴ b⁴   c⁵

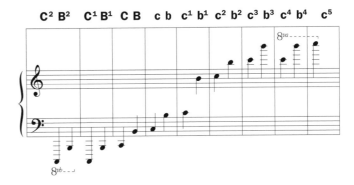

To continue to progress with the flute you might like to try these other great publications

GUEST SPOT

RESTART FLUTE CD TRACK LISTING

FULL INSTRUMENTAL PERFORMANCES

1. **WILLIAM TELL OVERTURE**
(ROSSINI)
DORSEY BROTHERS MUSIC LIMITED

2. **THE CAN CAN**
(OFFENBACH)
DORSEY BROTHERS MUSIC LIMITED

3. **MOON RIVER**
(MERCER/MANCINI)
SONY/ATV HARMONY UK

4. **THAT'S AMORÉ**
(WARREN/BROOKS)
PEERMUSIC (UK) LIMITED/SONY/ATV HARMONY UK

5. **THEME FROM *MISSION: IMPOSSIBLE***
(SCHIFRIN)
SONY/ATV HARMONY UK

6. **MORNING**
(GRIEG)
DORSEY BROTHERS MUSIC LIMITED

7. **HALLELUJAH**
(COHEN)
SONY/ATV MUSIC PUBLISHING (UK) LIMITED

8. **BIG SPENDER**
(FIELDS/COLEMAN)
CAMPBELL CONNELLY & CO. LIMITED

9. **THE LONELY GOATHERD**
(HAMMERSTEIN II/RODGERS)
IMAGEM MUSIC

10. **OYE COMO VA**
(PUENTE)
EMI MUSIC PUBLISHING LIMITED

11. **I GOT RHYTHM**
(GERSHWIN)
DORSEY BROTHERS MUSIC LIMITED

12. **SUPER TROUPER**
(ANDERSSON/ULVAEUS)
BOCU (ABBA) MUSIC/BOCU MUSIC LIMITED

BACKING TRACKS ONLY

13. **WILLIAM TELL OVERTURE**

14. **THE CAN CAN**

15. **MOON RIVER**

16. **THAT'S AMORÉ**

17. **THEME FROM *MISSION: IMPOSSIBLE***

18. **MORNING**

19. **HALLELUJAH**

20. **BIG SPENDER**

21. **THE LONELY GOATHERD**

22. **OYE COMO VA**

23. **I GOT RHYTHM**

24. **SUPER TROUPER**